THE ENGLISH BOAT

THE ENGLISH BOAT

Poems by Donald Revell

Alice James Books

FARMINGTON, MAINE

alicejamesbook.org

10 9 8 7 6 5 4 3 2 1

Alice James Books are published by Alice James Poetry Cooperative, Inc., an affiliate of the University of Maine at Farmington.

Alice James Books
114 Prescott Street
Farmington, ME 04938
www.alicejamesbooks.org

Names: Revell, Donald, 1954- author.
Title: The English boat / Donald Revell.
Description: Farmington, ME : Alice James Books, [2018]
Identifiers: LCCN 2017052420 (print) | LCCN 2017056882 (ebook) |
    ISBN 9781938584831 (eBook) | ISBN 9781938584763 (pbk. : alk. paper)
Classification: LCC PS3568.E793 (ebook) | LCC PS3568.E793 A6 2018
(print) |
    DDC 811/.54--dc23
LC record available at https://lccn.loc.gov/2017052420

Alice James Books gratefully acknowledges support from individual donors, private foundations, the University of Maine at Farmington, the National Endowment for the Arts, and the Amazon Literary Partnership.

ART WORKS.
arts.gov

amazon literary
partnership ✎

COVER ART: "Boat-Building near Flatford Mill" by John R.A. Constable. © Victoria and Albert Museum, London.

CONTENTS

ACKNOWLEDGMENTS

I wish to thank the editors of the following journals in which some of these poems first appeared:

The Ampersand Review
The American Poetry Review
The Cincinnati Review
Free Verse
Marsh Hawk Review
New American Writing
Plume
Poetry
The Poetry Review

For Gerald Stern

Now all is done; bring home the bride again

—Edmund Spenser

THE ENGLISH BOAT

LEONTES

Elusive, but only sweetened by
Disuse, souls I'd entered once before
Once again trouble the surfaces of life
With their small noises and single color...
Picture the dream before the last dream
Of a troubled night—something like that.

There were no survivors. Afterwards,
I meet them in weak sunlight in a corner
Of urban parkland. Not far away,
There seem to be children emerging
From the waters of an ornamental lake.
Swan boats lead them off to the horizon.

We are so happy. The sunlight grows weaker.
Reunion shakes the world. Let us speak of it.

PERICLES

What are my friends? Mouths, not eyes for
Bitterest underflesh of the farewell.
I was a man and suffered like a girl.
I spoke underneath to where the lights are

Pretty, pretty, pretty whence they came to tell
One God gets another. My friends are
Mouths for God, tearing me. In such a world
Broken only daughter opens to splendor.

My first thought was that dying is a deep well
Into the image of death, a many of one girl.
Later it meant to smile with no face where
Mirrors are mouths. Cupid and Psyche wore

Blindfolds made of glass, which explains why girls
Get to Heaven early mornings Adam fell.
Gods after gods we go. Still later,
Friends shouldered high mountains to the lee shore.

Gashed, and the gash a fountain of waters,
The landscape defames a single flower:
Amaranth. Magic hides an island world
Of boys and one daughter. I buried a pearl

In God's eye. And yet He sees her,
Defames her, considers His time well
Spent imagining a continent of flowers
Whose final climate is a broken girl.

Bells of a Cretan woman in labor
Hurled from a tower, flesh realer
Than the ground she somehow upwards curled
Into the bloom of her groin where bells

Are bees. I am an old man with a new beard.
I am the offspring of my child sprung from Hell.
Shipwreck makes peninsular metaphor
Out of my hatred, her rape, and one bell tower.

Confusion suicides the poems, Heaven I heard
Where the juice runs from stone-struck flowers.
At the end of the world I must use proper
Violence. Nothing is more true to tell.

Tell the taut-strung higher calendars
I've a margent in mind and new words
Hope to say, catastrophe to hear,
Old confederates and inwood apples

Where apples never shone. Also tell
Of mountains shouldered underneath one flower
Called amaranth. They tired of the world
Who made the world this way. God never

Did, never will. If you were to call
From the bottom of the ocean, the words,
Every one to me a living daughter,
Would shout wild mercy as never was before.

UTAH

In Memory of Sundin Richards

For a certainty…the worrying doves
Not of eyesight, but small as of a hand
Reaching inside her one last time:
The wise child, the foreshortened moment then.

Pulling the green out of her trees with heat,
Her eyesight, small between the wings, is wet.
Is wet, like a certain town in the trees.
I had built it, a free man's jubilo,

Upwards as a hornet in the blue, for
Certainty. Tell me that the boy loves more
The more deeply his hand, the smaller she.
I shall answer with blind eyes. Say to me

The boy was climbing to his worried dove.
I shall answer without Christ, just this once.

DEVOTION

For the main road and shortest road to heaven is run by
desires and not by footsteps.
—The Cloud of Unknowing

The spoken wish for a violin
Ermine of eighteen identical cypresses
Jagged index visionary without law
God's signature Mary's human impress

Last ruined tenant of these human walls
Vein of broken petals buried deeply
One smoke one shingle steaming in Muir Woods
Sharp morning in the pines' tall secrecy

Cloud an eye inward from heaven directly
Eye originally a walking sunflower
American inward Kansas either end
Shawnee Mission love's sign upon a calendar

Accurate music wedding mechanics
Small preaching in the bodies of animals
Me and a quantity of my handseled altars
Horses St. Agnes' hurricane the perils

Acrobats adorable pure music
Heaped logarithms white state of books
Stolen cameras madhouse just next door
Through the woods mad by thieving looks

Upstairs easel naked to lilacs still
A month until stolen Christ the wedding
Inaccurate inaccurate miracle
At Cana either end in narrow beds

Straight path along the dusky path homewards
Ordinariness spent no otherwise
Labor and bafflement without ending
Green corduroy copper hair then eyes

Wild with tangling underwood pleasure
In the dimness of the stars' pleasure
Pierced to the heart things said things said
Homlihed out of honey into Chaucer

Christ of bees babe of swarms weak not vacant
Winter when music when fires in vacant
Rail yard ashcans heavenly life beholden
One whole obdurate English for all saints

Audible ransom jokes and roses first
Snowdrop celandine a smaller fist
The rose her breast where the snow first
To infant now inclined now wholly kissed

The too-soft snow *homlihed* too-soft cider
Thaw to passion image on a veil
Vermeil as the Baroque much later
Bridal crown of bells shyly her regalia

Beautiful things new for the surprise
Of sky-children Christ but one of the names
In our lips the hush upon a pageant
Babe in arms bedded one last star the wain

Manhattan Island crèche of battlements
Almost a man-sized bramble dogwood
Away to the high places girls grown old
In miniver yet the neighborhood

Watchword tatterdemalion piety
True as true the pageant not ended
Dogwood actual tree for suicides
Bramble of men Mary's not mended

Manhattan inward cloister either end
Resurrection a walking linen
Love's ensign clean above the battlements
Churching aftertimes two worse men

Two horsemen Kentucky bred as alpine
Lovemaking somewhere close to the park
Suffrutescent in white union
A thin imagined by mountains the stark

Contrast not mine but cunning a dove
Imagined by mountains into this bed
Human impress ruined tenant of one love
Her lying down heart yet undivided

Mary so hush a mask so accurate
Corduroy spoken wish a violin
You the index signature the white state
Handseled without law cunning in Binghamton

Sugar hurricane high the road slow the walk
When lovely woman times three to *auld lang syne*
Why then ill nurses the bodies of animals
A debt to Beddoes the ruined heart of mine

Gone for a saint far from Little Cottonwood
Gone for a *cinéaste* far from me
Gone for an ugly girlfriend well-beloved
Vein of broken petals buried deeply

All in the waiting in the glass meanwhile
Adorable pure music of one side
Eyes downcast all the way to Heaven
How possibly handseled my rose bride

How possibly aftermath the F major
No one remaining the dead air
Cunning as semen Christ wagered
Christ livid aftermath her broken hair

As clear as elemental diamond
Or serene morning air far beyond
Secrecy at Cana one whole obdurate
Human his beautiful manners gone

Watteau upwards from the wedding feast
Never again such fragrances as these
No such accurate incense the least
Fingermark a fire in ambergris

A single violent transplant a torn ship
Emblem of the ark and strength of His name
Unchanged dead leaf in the owlet light
The endless happiness of my own name

FRESH DANTE

As of noon today is not one
Cell of mine, Toulouse, the eleventh
March 2001 ever lain with you
By Verdi's *Requiem*, the audience
Only now arriving, the kiddies left
Freely to play where Garonne
Is thick as paint at noon today, winter.

It comes over the radio.
It is wax fruit.
Not a saint but is footnoted,
Not one cell of mine
But ermines berries in a bowl.
Virtuosity of the half man shames
The concert master ever since you.
Fiddle & bow man, burial fruit
For Gabriel and Judas footnoted,
Play against myself to lie with you.

Berries are nice, Lady.
Grishkin is nice, Lullay.
The soul of Toulouse rots through.
Creation is one way. Creation
Is the other way too.

They have wedged cathedrals between bookstalls.
Between the edge of your sex and alto
France gapes. It spills out of you.
All the way from hoopla, colors
Drown the angel and hoist Judas.

West-running rivers are hopeless.
It's a shame to miss an hour even.
I mean an hour of saintliness.
As of noon tomorrow, not one
Cell of mine requiems anywhere.
Color me a maiden berry underneath.
Winter was the least of it.

THE PARLOR CITY

What'f…and I could go on saying
Little perfections now and then
Recalled (recauled) as I could say
At leisure the little movie palace
Around the corner from our place
Endicott NY wading up to her chin
Honeysuckle
                    Beau Cheval
                                Cider Mill
Wading up to sexy in fragrances
Scott Fitzgerald last of the belles
And Allen Tate's perfections cauled
Confederate dead in a Union town…

So many years have passed high time
We turned away as if from wedding vows
In a loose vein of broken petals
Beau cheval given away girls
Being strangers now

ARRAS

Bees as small, easily
Mistaken for sunlight
Now, as if again
The speed of light
Were mysterious, a thing
Unaccountable as this
Small bird, this emerald
Alighted on my reading glasses.

Two actual rivers:
One is of no use,
And it defines the soul
Of a nation; the other
Flows out to the world
Where the speed of light
Is nothing of bees as small,
Oh seasons, oh chateaux.

THE PIANO LESSON

For Karla Kelsey

A few notes, like planets of the remaining
Color, hunger here, sated only by distance,
Only by distance sated. There are no cabs.

Our Spaniard, perhaps as near as the next room,
Would bellow pathos into the gash where child
Keeps his eye. Wise child. Tenderness is not
For such, not for lions. We stare across

The music, meeting you there, planets
Of laundry and an iron tree, green for Christmas.
I have invented a simple balcony for you

Behind the piano. Even in daylight,
There stands a soul against the rail. Her toque
Is thrown into the traffic noise. A few notes,
Yellow as tender to the sun, hang there.

A CHAPLET FOR MARY: SIX FLOWERS

Hire swyre is wittore than the swon

I

Agony was shy once, was solid ransom.
This very room entails the sun.
Author for other side, for see, make blind
The persuasion of every mind but mine.

I am angry to be alone with you.
Absence that overflows all blue flowers
Covers their false eyes, covers them blue.
I thought it only a matter of some few hours.

My bad. As I had never thought before,
The classics are there because sin is there.
I bank upon the color of clear eyes,
Hers, once upon a time. Away up, nickel-dime

Mary, in my very room, looks down.
My enemies starve to see her still my own.

I I

Metropolitan oval who's to know
Below the elevated trains
Expressive water-lights fatal sister
Her bangle a boy's eye a ruby
One death at Christmas everybody knows

Metropolitan oval who's to say
The jeweler was a dead man
A ring size repeated unto everlasting
When the angels were gone away
So far as far as water freezes

Ellipses to magnify true Jesus
Still to come his assurance his late train
I am the boy my eye is upon him
A ruby so far as Mary pleases

III

Not the star, but homely grace and an accustomed tree
Guided the three of them. As if earth itself
Were a slender, tenacious grip upon coldest air.
Soil grew upward into trees. Uncanny grace
Was a broken, white-necked swan who birthed alone
God alive at the foot of a tree in the mess there.

History consents to the miracle because
It must, just as a sandstorm of atoms in Asia
Settles into the form of wings. Yet Asia
Has no wings and not any altars underground.
With God's help, we have oppressed them with our wealth.
With God's help, they will now revenge themselves with
    numbers.
I sing of Mary climbed out of earth alive.

I V

The apparition of a living rainbow,
Primeval motley of the first clowns
Where time is wrists upon a cloud,
Carries the horologe a hair's breadth unto
Mary. Obsolete is as far as I go.

Archaic are the girls on mountainsides.
Martha gathering flowers gathers
Colors for the afterlife. A white
Primeval motley apparitions my father's
One son. Wouldn't you like to know?

Wouldn't you like to set fire to time itself,
Like a Chinese pig? Obsolete is proud.
Bellflowers skirt about the girls themselves.
Purple rampion measured the Christ so.

V

There came a time the owls caught fire,
So many Florentines the lamps
Failed in tall waters priestcraft failed.
White of lime and no languages
Captured the owls that caught fire.

Mary is the mother of God.
No less kind of love or craving
Sharp briars, her primrose food,
Hurts her. Weary so water say
The feather of her is past saving.

Imagine a chapel smaller
Than a pebble. In walks fire,
White of lime into apple shape
In childbirth, so much cold.
Wild bends low, fire onto feather.

VI

What more should Heaven
Be than white litter
Of desert willows on
The long June grass?

I am not injured.
My son is in peril
Though I want for nothing.
Birds in litter. Birds.

Heaven, a help to no one,
Helps me. Once more
Greensward look me
In the eye! Out of

The setting moon a keen
Wind seeks the sun,
The sun's face. Find
Me a suicide, and in

The face of such peril
I want for nothing.
What more could Heaven
Allow or broken pencil

Of the Holy Ghost write
Now? Inward my son.
The women are birds there
On real grass. Nakedness

Litters the air with rescue.
Take it. Wrap it round
Fat and lymph and bone.
God sometimes knows his own.

RAPTURE

Time might be anything, even the least
Portion of shadow in the blaze, that helpless
Hare of darkness in the hawk's world.
I'd forgotten, in the haste of me, to reach
Backwards into time one hand. Come along.
I've seen a rainbow where no rain ever was.
The colors were slain children of the wind
Alive again because time might be anything,
And earth a broken astrolabe
Plunged into blackness by force of sunlight
These latter days. There is a flower
In the hawk's mouth once was an animal.
It hurries towards the sun, and the hawk,
Helpless in the color of it, becomes rain.

TAPPAN ZEE: FURS FOR A RIVER

The secret oar and petals of all love.
—Hart Crane

I

Perfect knowledge offers the man a bowl
Beautifully painted inside with lilacs.
Where the flowers divide from their stems
Little cracks show heart-shaped leaves,
And deep among them something like
Ermine for the murdered republic looks
Alive, looks to be the fur of stones
By a waterfall. He is a small man,
Writing as quickly as he can. Alewives
Come to mind, as do the wide children
Of the Hudson River School. If you
Are my son and reading this, stop. Run
Berries underwater and fill the bowl
Until no flowers show. Make me an offer.

II

His hands were anxious to be hands,
Incomprehensible, not restful.
Travel your eyes to a thin branch,
There for to see death twinned to sail.
Whoosh, children! Whirlybirds
Frisk in the ermine autumn mind,
Death's twinning. Anxious hands
Make tea whose color, fitful,
Whose savor bays October moon.
I love the past for hating you.
I love my hands for their taper. Two
Hands worried this summer past
Nearly to death. Whoosh, we live forever!
The trees are Norway maples even there.

III

Ermine elate
As strayed into a low garden
Where ghosts shelter in courtesy
Never again to be seen
Soon or late
It might have been Manhattan
As the island was in 1970
When freedom was a machine
White elated

I have come to reject destiny as completely as I reject death
It is unnatural this dying this walking over the heads of
    specters
For a certainty transformation is the fur and engine of all
    death
Else nothing is explained no pair of birds alive in our
    Manhattan
In the wake of courtesy finding a low place fallen from the sun

IV

It ermines berries in a bowl taller
To the west.
To the west the bridge commends
Idylls, needles,
But no true river
Tall as obscenity when every word
Is obscene, a man my age.

The apples! But the taste is ermine,
Miniver, or
Rather say an Irishman is dying
To show the boy,
And I go unhurt, with afterwards
A bowl to show.
We crossed the bridge in time for the ball game.

CONFESSIO AMANTIS

It is correct to love even at the wrong time.
—Spencer Reece, "ICU"

1.

Remaining only,
As though a tree had fashioned calendars,

Things to be written
Slowly, cautiously if ever at all—

Scent of his semen
On her mouth, 1000 and more flowers

Allow for music,
The tang of distraction from violence.

We savaged the boy,
As he had savaged the least among us.

The truth of flowers
Sped from his wounds, becoming girls and soil,

Atalanta, yes,
After all these years her broken sandal

Is a pure nation
Whence I come to this extreme of caution.

Spark of the nighthawk
Begins a blaze of constellations, none

So fast a runner.
If my body breeds 1000 flowers,

As does your body
Lifted like a sweetened sponge on a spear

Leaning in to kiss
What? This flesh of ours is a last tasting

Before the last dream
Ends, my hands finding your hands in the blaze.

2.

Remaining only,
As though a willow had suicided

Girls equal to Christ
In the upended, in the upheld shade,

Thin film of themselves
Upon which I project an image made

Of sweetness living
To bitter death which created me.

Is there room at all
For the girlish Christ, the aside wild tree?

Abandoned to clouds
Of dark bees, sponge-sweet uplifted spear points,

All the living man
Or God could ever really have wanted

Rips the physical
World to pieces, apocalypse darling.

I abandoned you
In summer's heat and basement piano.

Children rip the world
And then the leaf falls, the August meadow

Fills with dark water.
Missouri was our Aulis and daughter.

Cautiously, slowly,
American rivers in new systems

Seek disgrace and love,
New babes afloat are all the emblems of.

3.

Fire I cannot reach
Begin a blaze of constellations, each

More hawk than before,
Speed like semen the remaining music,

Like ruined airplanes
Into buildings to purpose new nations

Of colorless boys.
If as you say you say, come from the cross

Down to this sweetness.
1000 and more flowers reek your wounds:

Violets calmly,
And daisies by jokes, roses, final friends.

Where does caution end?
I have folded two lives into one life

And an only son
Into a tale of mermen surfacing,

Sexpools and coral
Telling granite to move, the red rock move.

Used to be I knew
America. At nightfall, trees turned blue.

4.

I have taken fright.
Antiquated expression perfectly

Suited Tappan Zee,
A girl's throat, the white angel of a bridge

Sexing the waters.
Caution begins with the last words of Christ.

The extreme of hawk,
The cloud of true bees that is a new babe,

Savage as savage,
Shatters a bird in the wheel well, wheel well.

I beg your pardon.
For whom betrayal is sacramental,

Wheel well, wheel well, white
Angel of the bridge meaning to flower

In death, forgive me.
My harms are voices thrown into the trees.

The soft vow Mary
Tendered to the angel was none of these.

Her vow was berries
In the scent of berries and on the leaves.

A cloud in Tallis
Spem in Alium between the timbers,

In a black smother
Her vow forgave, suddenly, entity.

As earth's honor was,
My harm's mortal, faithless circle of trees

Closed around a girl
Whose lily hand was closed. The harm is me.

5.

Old men are changed men,
Prone to days of nothing but early morning,

Evening retrograde.
And one who imagined circles of men,

Son of the morning,
Has driven a broken vow through my heart.

For the good to know:
A naked thinking heart that makes no show

Hangs in the window.
Such things are nothing left to say, although

Slowly, cautiously,
A winter is coming when we shall crawl the sky.

The ideal farewell
To Atalanta, for the good to know,

And even in milk
I find the sinews of farewell to her,

Is the entity
Lifted by flowers and bees to her mouth

And to Jesus' mouth.
My amends make no music after all.

I savaged a boy.
I fed 1000 flowers from his wounds.

The hair of the hour
Was joyful noise restoring the pure sound

Of all English words.
Old poets grow quiet, loving all words

Equally, all red
Hair, all the names they might conjure for love.

Walking, tongues, and feet
Make for traffic at the foot of the cross.

His wounds overflow.
There is nothing good to say for pathos.

Tenderness only
Matters, semen of flowers and of bees.

6.

Remaining only
Naked Atalanta, hobbled but tall,

In direct sunlight
Walking out of the underwood and small

Copper-colored trees
Onto the black expressway to be killed.

The hawk's contention
Is that tenderness trumps pathos always.

The hawk on fire
Hunts among the lapwings, a cloud of saints

Assumed in their skins
Naked to Heaven, hobbled but alive.

Begun in a blaze
Of constellations and calendars, my

Confession to hair
Here in my mouth, dark hair, 1000 days

Of words I should say
Slowly, cautiously if ever at all—

Comes now my darling.
No one I have ever harmed deserved harm.

The fault in my stars
Was hammered there by me, in love's despite.

I sheltered nothing
But ill will from ill will and wind, white thoughts

From whiteness itself.
Still, there is no evil worth the telling.

The world is perfect.
Unaccountably, in the midwinter,

The sun will hurry
Down to mountains of new soil and soft trees.

HOMAGE TO SAMUEL DANIEL: EIGHT SONNETS

When we hear music we must be in our ear, in the utter-room of sense
—Samuel Daniel, "A Defence of Rhyme" (1603)

While owls were still about the roads
Came time and the strong, silly notion
Of our not being at war in the whispers.

Age dreads weather, any of it. The unnoticed
Leaf hurries home ahead of rain,
Ahead of the sun that feeds it, killing it.

Age dreads. Also a dream came, owls
Whispering the names of a secret river.
Telltale Johnny puzzles maps

With rain the wrong color, water
Falling where it ought to rest. Leaf
Has the eyes for it and good speed.

Take from these Classics new arms, old eyes,
Omens. Watchword is the road to rise.

Can they improve the sky? I saw
A grin without a cat, one Esau
Messing with meteors where starlings meant
To stitch the clouds together for Jacob's tent.

None of this is old.
Boys with beards are nevertheless
Not old.
I consider the desperation
Of one bird in two trees and, whoosh!
Terrors, a death-sweat of grapes,
Streak the cold heaven.
I'm old, but none of this is old.
You have dreamt it, draped it, and so have I.

Starlings shrilled a new sound onto the sky.

In the blue ship's wake, a coronal
Of white birds, trying to live, lives.
Say for a certainty, even one final
Time, truly what I know. Forgiveness
Pilots the colors. And so the colors live.

Creatures first to last we die
In perfect cotillion.
I was made here. Farther, my
Adventures got a son.

Tend to him, tend to him. Braid a coronal.
A white bird stops a while in the boy.
Say for a certainty, even one final
Safe return, that truth is underway
In goodly spindrift and the blue ship's wake.

Small woods upon an incline
Thewed of the Levin, lean
Down there exactly trodden
Where leaves become a hillside torrent
To a broken man a small dog
In the crook of his arm. Imagine
He carries a windmill
In a walnut shell, imagine
Across the bivouacs of Labrador
One Samuel loves one hotter
A virgin to the last of men
All onto the shining grass, eagles,
Onto the fallen leaves a Prophet,
The glory and misfortune of angels here.

God was no poet and then was.
In the spring of '65 I walked inland
Along Middletown Road towards the trains
Speeding through the sky and with canals
Turbid on each side, water traffic then,
Low barges painted yellow and black men
Waving upwards to the bridge keepers.

Sometimes churches, sometimes brittle scented trees.
Red lanceolate, brittle leaves and almost
Lilac any girl at all the mother of God,
Grail legend, outlandish tabloids. I say this:
The spirit of tolerance requires
No one to be stupid, no one at all. Son
And heir, fire, air, the world is flawless.

A mad, favorite flower was left.
To write, it is necessary to write.
For love to continue the beehive
A commune must sing and must believe.

These western states get slowed down,
Their sarabands plowed right under.
I begin to think my shadow divorced
Another man, a man before me, and left

Us two together in a low, white woodland.
Shirt to shirt, shrill ballooning, we pooled
Buttons unbuttoned where my heart should be.
The American poem was still good.

I saw a fence-line of strange uniform
Becoming bees, favorites of mine.

Of youth-time itself—say Adirondack, Berkshire, Ktaadn—
Enigmas guessed at instantly, once upon a time,
I am clinging to the torches of it all, white phalloi
Upheld, flowers walking unaided over rugged
Soil. Henry Thoreau was neither childish nor childlike.
He was a real boy. He guessed instantly arrowheads,
Panopticons to find a missing house and the poor hanged girl.
Our youth is obscure only where it is rational.
Louisa cut hair. Attaboy, and sends Honduras packing.
My God, my King, these pictures are free for the taking.
With two young eyes, white flowers could walk all the way
Home under God, humanly. Eden's the living end.
When the Modern was a boy and wild for it, one size fit all.
Here in America, we hang pictures on the walls.

It is only recently the faces
In dreams became unrecognizable.
I live in a haze and sleep perfectly
Among strangers. How can you talk to people
Who don't know anything, have never read
Anything? Dream, dream, dream. As I just said
To the most beautiful woman over there
In the white hair with coronal as clear
As though each wet petal of each flower
Were glass, *I have never seen you before.*
There are no words where there is no color.
There is only the reply beyond dreams,
A west-running river fed by clear streams
And torchlights setting the water ablaze.

THE GLENS OF CITHAERON

Till the gold fields of stiff wheat
Cry "We are ripe, reap us!"
—Ted Hughes

I begin to think Actaeon never changed.
The words that followed him, the poems
That leapt upon him and left him for dead
Were difficult exactly to the extent
They were rational. It makes perfect sense
For nakedness to give way to frenzy.
And the poems, let's be clear, were naked.

Time was, questions were put, clear as water.
The Goddess bathed, and time was the soft smile
Of water catching the sunlight on her.
And the sunlight, let's be clear, was sheer murder.
Into the same creature, no human word
Leaps twice. Given to frenzy, nakedness
Smiles upon the breaking of men and dogs.

How easy to lose all patience with chaste things!
Lord, I am hoping to hear from you
Before the hunters and suicides make off with me.
Lord, I am hoping to take your weapons
To a tarn freezing in the death of me.
I shall harry the moon there. I shall halloo.
Bayed in the crosstree is a lion too.

In 1969 a red stag made
A cobweb of moonlight in his antlers.
For once in your life, pray without ceasing.
Pray the stag safely past the lion's tree.
Actaeon never changed. Predator
Is simply prey to nakedness and reason.
The poems have been out hunting all the time.

Then it is Friday. Frisk. You might as well.
Seeing as the rapeweed, you might as well.
The lion is no stranger. The belling
Stag is as familiar as the moon, but a strange
Suicide. Taken by legs, taken
By sinews, kissing the cobwebs of moonlight,
He prays the prayer I was not quick to say.

Berries and hoardings, ermine horseplay short
Of the new, short of poems no longer old
As I knew them, leaving the small schools
For the main campus rapeweed climbing, pale.
It is Friday. Stars won't cross. Actaeon
Never imagined the frail, sheer speed
Of meat. Lord, eat me. Nothing else makes sense.

On the far
Safe side of becoming,
Metaphor

Is all love,
The pure being of each
Nude above

Perfect sense.
I begin to hunt words.
The tension

The soft smile
Of the Goddess eases
A short while

Reappears
In a red stag's terror.
Metaphor

Leaps and eats.
It is not difficult.
Love is meat.

The dogs leap on Actaeon. He is human.
I begin to think of Time as anything
In the gift of humans or as sacrifice
To the long uplift of lions in the blood.
Now dogs tear deeply into the living flesh.
Each moment is a visible agony,
And still the godly human nature remains

Unharmed. I never imagined the sheer frail
Of fear so powerful. Legs and sinews turn
Into flowers. Between her breasts, the Goddess
Shelters one such, one blood violet alive.
The porch of Heaven is littered with color.
As familiar as the moon, our humanness
Crosses into heaven as the new poem.

On the far side of becoming, a life's work
Begins another kind of work, but naked
Of change. There are animals, water, and trees.
Nothing is recognizable in its old
Skin, yet everything shimmers. I am afraid,
Shrinking from the teeth of the cold water
And from the howling trees. I perish at this point

Down among dogs and upwards beside lion.
The pieces of me are carried fast away
By plot and rhyme. See Artemis bathing.
The moonlight on her body is the mother
Of God. It makes perfect sense. I am eaten
And fed changeless into her breast, blood
Violet alive. I remain your friend.

BOOK BENEFACTORS

Alice James Books wishes to thank the following individual who generously contributed toward the publication of *The English Boat:*

Anonymous

For more information about AJB's book benefactor program, contact us via phone or email, or visit alicejamesbooks.org to see a list of forthcoming titles.

RECENT TITLES FROM ALICE JAMES BOOKS

A L I C E   J A M E S   B O O K S has been publishing poetry since 1973. The press was founded in Boston, Massachusetts as a cooperative wherein authors performed the day-to-day undertakings of the press. This collaborative element remains viable even today, as authors who publish with the press are also invited to become members of the editorial board and participate in editorial decisions at the press. The editorial board selects manuscripts for publication via the press's annual, national competition, the Alice James Award. AJB remains committed to its founders' original mission to support women poets, while expanding upon the scope to include poets of all genders, backgrounds, and stages of their careers. In keeping with our efforts to foster equity and inclusivity in publishing and the literary arts, AJB seeks out poets whose writing possesses the range, depth, and ability to cultivate empathy in our world and to dynamically push against silence. The press was named for Alice James, sister to William and Henry, whose extraordinary gift for writing went unrecognized during her lifetime.

Designed by Mike Burton

Printed by McNaughton & Gunn